CONTENTS

SYMPHONY NO. 3 IN C MINOR ("Organ"), Op. 78 (*ca.* 1886)

INSTRUMENTATION

3 Flutes (Flute 3 doubles Piccolo) [Flûte, Fl.; 3e Flûte (Grand Fl.) ou Petite (Pte.) Fl.]
2 Oboes [Hautbois, Hb.]
English Horn [Cor Anglais, Cor. Ang.]
2 Clarinets in B♭ [Clarinettes, Cl. (Si♭)]
Bass Clarinet in B♭ [Clarinette Basse, Cl. B. (Si♭)]
2 Bassoons [Bassons, Bons.]
Contrabassoon [Contrebasson, C. Bon.]

2 Horns in C, E♭, E [Cors (Ut, Mi♭, Mi)]
2 Horns *(chromatic)* in F [Cors. *(chrom.)* (Fa)]
2 Trumpets in F [Trompettes, Tromp. (Fa)]
Trumpet *(natural)* in C [Trompette, Tromp. *(naturelle)* (Ut)]
3 Trombones [Trombones, Tromb.]
Tuba [Tuba]

Timpani [Timbales, Timb.]
Triangle [Triangle]
Cymbals & Bass Drum [Cymbales (Cymb.) et Grosse Caisse (Gsse. Csse.)]

Organ [Orgue]
Piano *(2 and 4 hands)* [Piano *(à 4 mains)*]

Violins 1, 2 [Violons]
Violas [Altos]
Cellos [Violoncelles, Velles.]
Basses [Contrebasses, C. B.]

GLOSSARY OF FRENCH TERMS IN THE MUSIC

changer en Ut, change to the C instrument [horns]
divisés (en 4, etc.), divisi (in 4 parts, etc.)
en, in
et, and
étouffez, damp [the triangle and cymbal]
Fa, F-natural
fin, end
La♭, A♭
même valeur de mesure, same time value
Mi, E-natural
Mi♭, E♭
Péd[ale], pedal of the organ
sans nuance (aux Contrebasses), without shading (in the Basses)
sans presser, unhurried
Si♭, B♭
Sol, G-natural
sons bouchés, stopped ("choked") sounds [horn]
une Cymbale frappée avec une baguette, one cymbal struck with a stick
une mesure comme trois du mouv[emen]t précédent, one measure equals the value of three preceding measures
Ut, C-natural

Organ, p. 64: "voix céleste" ("celestial voice") and "32 pieds" ("32-foot stop") are standard French organ registrations.

SYMPHONY NO. 3
("Organ")
in Full Score

Camille Saint-Saëns

DOVER PUBLICATIONS, INC.
New York

Published in Canada by General Publishing Company, Ltd., 30 Lesmill Road, Don Mills, Toronto, Ontario.
Published in the United Kingdom by Constable and Company, Ltd., 3 The Lanchesters, 162–164 Fulham Palace Road, London W6 9ER.

Bibliographical Note

This Dover edition, first published in 1994, is an unabridged republication of *3e Symphonie en ut mineur par Camille Saint-Saëns, Op. 78*, originally published by Durand et Schœnewerk, Éditeurs, Paris, n.d. The Dover edition adds lists of contents and instrumentation, and a glossary of French terms in the music.

Library of Congress Cataloging-in-Publication Data

Saint-Saëns, Camille, 1835–1921.
[Symphony no. 3, op. 78, C minor]
Symphony no. 3 : ("Organ") / Camille Saint-Saëns.—In full score.
1 score.
Originally published: Paris : Durand et Schœnewerk.
ISBN 0-486-28306-2 (pbk.)
1. Symphonies—Scores.
M1001.S154 op. 78 1994 94-17028
CIP
M

Manufactured in the United States of America
Dover Publications, Inc., 31 East 2nd Street, Mineola, N.Y. 11501

To the memory of Franz Liszt

SYMPHONY NO. 3 IN C MINOR
("Organ") Op. 78 (*ca.* 1886)

I.

Adagio 76 =
1.e Flûte
2.e Flûte
3.e Flûte (ou P.te Flûte)
Grande Fl
2 Hautbois
1°
1 Cor Anglais
2 Clarinettes en SI♭
1 Clarinette Basse en SI♭
2 Bassons
1 Contrebasson
1.er et 2.e Cors en UT
3.e et 4.e Cors (chrom.) en FA
1.re et 2.e Trompettes en FA
3.e Trompette en UT
1.er et 2.e Trombones
3.e Trombone et Tuba
Timbales
Orgue
Adagio 76 =
Violons
Altos
Violoncelles
Contrebasses

Allº moderato 72=♩.
Cor Ang.
p
pp
Bons
1º
p
pp
Timb.
pp
Allº moderato 72=♩.
p
p
p
Velles et C.B.
pizz.
p poco marcato
arco
Cl.
1º
p
Bons
1º
p
1er et 2e Cors
pp
Timb.

1re Fl.
2e Fl.
3e Fl.
Hb 1o
p cresc.
f
mf
Cor Ang.
p cresc.
Cl.
Cl. B. p cresc.
Bons
p
C. Bon
Cors
3o
cresc.
Tromp.
Tromb.
Timb.
Col C.B.

A
p
dim.
à 2
pp
Col C.B.
A

1º
p
pp
pizz.

1º
3º
pizz.
pizz.

B
cresc.
p cresc.
f
à 2
Div.
arco
pizz.

p
cresc.
mf
dim.
arco
f
Col C.B.

8
f
dim.
mf
p
pp
tr
fp
arco

Cor Ang.
mf espress.
Bons 1o
mf espress.
1er et 2e Cors
pp
Timb.
pp
Velles et C.B.
C
1re Fl.
mf espress.
sf
Hb. 1o
mf espress.
sf
Cor Ang.
Cl. 1o
mf espress.
sf
Cl. B.
mf espress.
sf
Bons
1er et 2e Cors
p
3e Tromp.
p
Timb.
p
C
Div.

1re Fl.
sf
2e Fl.
sf
Petite Fl.
mf
sf
sf
Hb
Cor Ang.
Cl.
mf
sf
Cl.B.
sf
Bons
C.Bon
mf
f
Cors
mf
f
Tromp.
2o
1o
p
Tromb.
p
Timb.
mf
sf
sf
mf
sf
sf

D
8
cresc.
sf
f
ff
mf
p
à 2
cresc. molto
p cresc. poco a poco

8
dim.
à 2
mf
sf
p
f

1º
dim.
legg.
p
p legg.
4º
mf
pp

Cl.
Bons
Timb.
pp
p
pizz.
Velles et C.B.
E
1re Fl.
2e Fl.
Grande Fl.
Hb. 1º
Cor Ang.
Bons sempre pp
3e et 4e Cors
Div.
arco

1re Fl.
2e Fl.
3e Fl.
Hb.
Cl.
Cl. B.
Bons
3e et 4e Cors
F
pp
p
p espress.
3o
arco
mf
Velles et C.B.

1re Fl.
p espress
2e Fl.
3e Fl.
Hb
Cor Ang.
p espress.
Cl.
Cl. B.
Bons
à 2
C. Bon
Cors
Tromp.
Tromb.
Timb.
sempre p
sempre p

1º
3º p
4º p
3º
1º
dim.
dim.
Col C.B.

G
mf
dim.
p
1º
1º pp
3º pp
Divisés
en 4
pp

cresc.
à 2
1º
p
tr
Div. en 2
Col C.B.

Petite Fl.
à 2
cresc.
Unis.
Col C.B.

sf
sf
f
f
à 2
à 2
Col C.B.

ff
1º
Tuba
Col C.B.

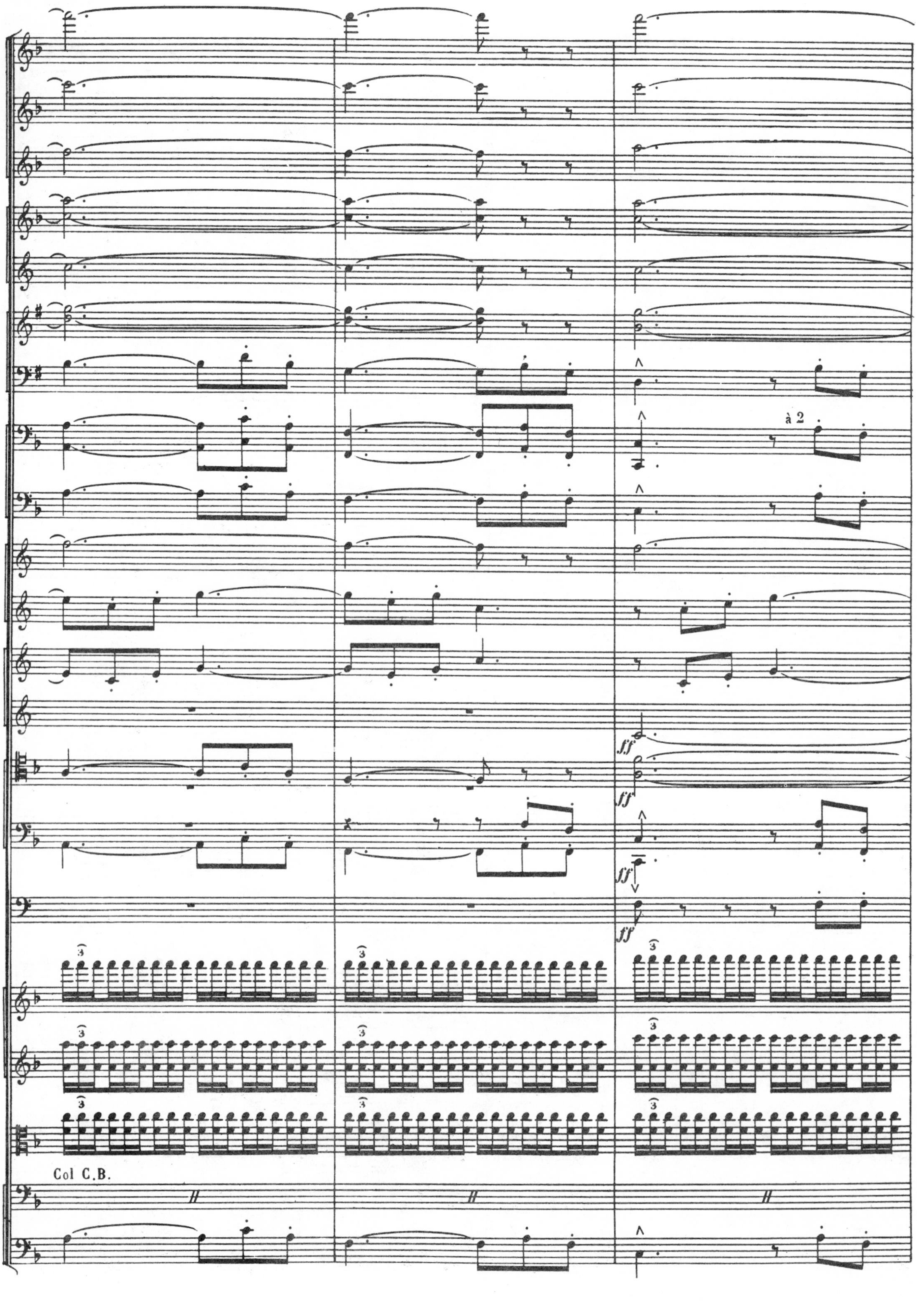
à 2
ff
ff
ff
ff
Col C.B.

H
à 2
à 2
ff
H
Col C.B.

dim.
mf
p
pp

Grande Fl.
pp
sf

I
sf
p
cresc.
f

1º
p
3º
p
pp
pp
pp
sf
pp
sf

J
pp
1º
J
Altos
Div.
Div.

tr
pp

Petite Fl.
1º
1º
à 2
tr
p

1º
à 2
cresc.
Div.
cresc.
cresc.
cresc.

mf
p
cresc.
1º
à 2
tr
Unis.

K
f
dim.
p
f
dim.
p
f
1º
mf
espress.
f
f
f
f
f
f
p
f
f
f
tr
f
K
f
dim.
p
2ds Vons
Div.
f
dim.
p
f
dim.
p
tr
f
dim.
p
Unis.
f
dim.
f
dim.
f
dim.

1°
p
cresc.
mf espres.
cresc.
cresc.
espres.
cresc.
cresc.
tr
tr
cresc.

cresc. molto
cresc. molto
cresc. molto
cresc. molto
a 2
1º cresc. molto
p
mf
cresc. molto
cresc. molto
cresc. molto
cresc. molto
p cresc. molto

L
sf
à 2
marc.
tr
dim.
p
f
Unis.

à 2
sf
à 2
sf
sf
sf
sf
sf

M
à 2
M sempre ff
Velles
Unis.
Div.

ff
ff
ff
à 2
ff
ff
à 2
ff

à 2
à 2
à 2
ff
à 2
ff
à 2
Unis.

N
à 2
N
sempre ff

sempre ff
à 2 sempre ff
sempre ff
à 2
sempre ff
à 2 sempre ff
Col C.B.

sempre ff
sempre ff
à 2
sempre ff
1º
sempre ff
sempre ff

Pte Fl.
à 2

8
dim.
mf
f
à 2
1º

1º
p legg.
p
legg.
4º
mf
dim.
pp
pizz. p

pp
pp
1º
pp
pp
sempre pp
pp
pp
pp

O
Div.
arco
(pizz)
arco
arco

1re Fl.
2e Fl.
Hb.
Cl. B.
Bons
C. Bons
Velles et C. B.
dim.
dim.
dim.
1re Fl.
Hb.
3e et 4e Cors
pp
pp
pp
Unis
sempre pp
arco
sempre pp
sempre pp
Velles
sempre pp
C.B.

1re Fl.
2e Fl.
Grande Fl.
3e et 4e Cors
4o
sempre pp
Div.
pizz.
arco
3e Fl.
P
Unis.

1re Fl.
pp
2e Fl.
pp
Hb
1o
pp
pp
Cl.
pp
Timb.
pp
dim.
pp
pizz.
dim.
pp
pizz.
dim.
pp
pizz.
dim.
pp
pizz.
Hb
1o pp
Bons
pp
1o

1º
pp
Bons
Velles et C.B.
pizz.
1er et 2e Cors
1º pp
pp
Poco adagio ♩=60
ORGUE
pp
Ped.
Poco adagio ♩=60
arco
pp
arco
pp
arco
pp
Velles
arco
pp
C.B.

pp
Q
Cl.
1º p
poco cresc.
3º et 4º Cors p
3º
poco cresc.
1er et 2e Tromb.
1º
p
poco cresc.
Q
pp
1ers Vons Div.
pp
pp
2ds Vons Div.
pp
pp
Altos Div.
pp
Velles Div.
C. B.

1re Fl.
2e Fl.
3e Fl.
Hb.
Cor Ang.
Cl.
Cl.B.
Bons
C. Bon
Cors
Tromp.
Tromb.
Timb.
Orgue
Ped.
R
Unis.
pp
p

Cl.
2e et 3e Cors
1er et 2e Tromb.
Orgue
sans nuance
Vons
Altos Div.
Vlles
C. B. Div.
sans nuance aux Contrebasses

Hb
Cor Ang.
Cl.
Cl.B.
Bons
C.Bons
Cors
Tromp.
Tromb.
Timb.
S
pp
tr

poco cresc.
Velles et C.B.
pp
pp
T
pp
Orgue
T
pp
Velles
pp
C.B.

poco cresc.
dim.
cresc.
dim.
1re Fl.
2e Fl.
3e Fl.
Hb
Cor Ang.
Cl.
Bons
pp
p
Col C.B.
molto tranquillo
pizz. p

1re Fl.
2e Fl.
3e Fl.
Hb.
Cor Ang.
Cl.
Cl. B.
Bons
C. Bon
Cors
Tromp.
Tromb.
Timb.
Orgue
pp
pizz.
p
pizz.
p
pizz.
p
Col C.B.

pp
Ped.
Div.
Col C.B.
cre
cresc.
cre - - - scen - - - do
cresc.

p cresc.
pp
pp (voix céleste)
32 pieds
arco
p molto espressivo
(pizz.)
cre - scen - do
Unis.
Div.

p 1º
p
1º
p
p
p
p
3º
p
poco cresc.
8
poco a poco cresc.
cresc.
cresc.
poco a poco cresc.
cresc.
poco a poco cresc.
cresc.
Div.
cresc.

p
p
p
dim.
pp
sf
sf
dim.
pp
dim.
pp
dim.
pp
pp
dim
pp
8
f
sempre f
dim. molto
f
dim.
dim. molto
f
dim.
dim. molto
f
sempre f
dim. molto
f
dim.
dim. molto
f
sempre f
dim. molto
f
dim.
dim. molto
Unis.
f
dim.
dim. molto

X
pp
arco
X
8

1º
pp

pp
2º
pp
pp
pp
pp
pp
cresc.
dim.
morendo
Altos Unis.
espress.
arco
pizz.

II.

All° moderato 80=♩.
1re Flûte
2e Flûte
Petite Flûte
2 Hautbois
Cor Anglais
2 Clarinettes en SI♭
Clarinette Basse en SI♭
2 Bassons
Contrebasson
1er Cor en MI♮
2e Cor en MI♭
3e et 4e Cors (chrom.) en FA
3e
2 Trompettes en FA
1 Trompette (naturelle) en UT
1er et 2e Trombones
3e Trombone et Tuba
3 Timbales
Triangle
Cymbales et Grosse Caisse
Orgue
Piano
All° moderato 80=♩.
Violons
Altos
Violoncelles
Contrebasses

à 2

f
f
f
f

A
8
p
à 2
poco marcato
A
pizz.
arco

8
cresc.
p cresc.
Col C.B.
f
p
1º

1re Fl.
2e Fl.
Hb.
Cor Ang.
Cl.
Bons
pizz.
arco
cresc.
Velles et C.B.

1re Fl.
2e Fl.
Pte Fl.
Hb
à 2
Cor Ang.
Cl.
Cl.B.
Bons
C.Bon
Cors
3o
Tromp.
Tromb.
Timb.
B
Col C.B.

cresc.
à 2
1ers Vons Div.
pizz.
arco
Unis.
2ds Vons Div.
Altos Div.

Col C.B.

8
1º
3º
C
rf
Col C.B.

8
1º
f
1º
3º
Col C.B.

f
3º
f
1º
3º
Col C.B.

1º
p
1º
p
p
f
p
brillante
p
Piano
Presto 138=
p

(en MI♭-UT-LA♭)
Triangle
D
1ers Vons Div.
2ds Vons Div.
pizz.
Col C.B.
pizz.

mf
mf
à 2
mf
mf
mf
1º
mf
mf
mf
Unis.
mf
Unis.
mf
arco
mf
Col C.B.
arco
mf

E
à 2
3º
Triangle
une Cymbale frappée avec une baguette
1ers Vons Div.
2ds Vons Div.
pizz.
Unis

cresc.
1º
cresc.
1º
1º
p
cresc.
arco
p
cresc.
cresc.
arco
p
cresc.
cresc.
cresc.

cresc.
cresc.
à 2
f
mf
p
3º
Triangle
Cymb.
F

1º
f
3º
mf
mf espress
mf espress.
Col C. B.

Div.
Div.
f

G
p
p
f
p
f
p
f
f
f
f
f
f
G
cresc.
f
pp
cresc.
f
pp
Unis.
f
pp
Unis.
cresc.
f
pp

poco a poco cresc.
p
poco a poco cresc.
poco a poco cresc.
poco a poco cresc.
p
p
p
pizz.
marcato
poco a poco cresc.
poco a poco cresc.
poco a poco cresc.
poco a poco cresc.
p poco a poco cresc.

rinf.
f
cresc.
à 2
mf
rinf
arco

H
à 2
1º
3º
en FA-UT-SOL
H
Col C.B.

I
tr
f
p
à 2
sf
1º
3º
f
I
rinf
p subito
p
rinf.

1º
p
1º
3º
p
p

cresc.
à 2
1°
3°

J
1º
Triangle
J
Div.
Div.
pizz.

K
cresc.
cresc.
cresc.
cresc.
à 2
p
1º
p
3º
p
K
cresc.
Unis
cresc.
Unis.
pizz
arco
cresc.
arco
pizz
cresc.

cresc.
p cresc.
à 2
à 2
cresc.
cresc.
cresc.
Piano
tr
pp
cresc.
cresc.
cresc.
arco
cresc.
cresc.

tr
f
1º
à 2
p
mf
8
Div.
cresc.
Unis.
ff

All.° mod.to 84 = ♩.
ff
f
3o
étouffez
étouffez
All.° mod.to 84 = ♩.

à 2
f
f
à 2
f
f
f

L
8
p
poco marcato
L
pizz.

8
cresc.
f
1º p
p
à 2
arco
Col C.B.

1re Fl.
2e Fl.
Hb
Cor Ang.
Cl.
Bons
Vons
pizz.
cresc.
arco

M
1re Fl.
2e Fl.
Petite Fl.
Hb.
à 2
Cor Ang.
Cl.
Cl. B.
Bons
Cors
3o
Tromp.
Tromb.
Timb.
Tr.
Cymb.
M

sf
p
cresc.
à 2
1ers Vons
Div.
pizz.
2ds Vons
Altos
p pizz.
cresc

Col C.B.
arco

8
8
Col C.B.
rf
rf
rf
rf
rf
rf
rf
rf

N
8
8
1º
f
N
Col C.B.

8
8
f
3º
f
1º
3º
Col C.B.

O
Presto 138=
1º
3º Tromb. et Tuba
O
Presto 138=
Col C.B.

1º
mf
1º
à 2
p
p
p
p
Col C.B.

Triangle
Piano
Col C.B.

mf
à 2
p
p
f
Col C.B.

P
f
à 2
p
cresc.
Div.
Altos Div.
Col C.B.

Cymb.
Piano
Col C.B.

Q
1º
f
f
8
Q
pizz.
f
pizz.
f
f
f
f
Col C.B.
f

1re Fl.
2e Fl.
Cor Ang.
Cl.
Bons
arco
pizz.
arco
pizz.
Velles et C.B.
Velles et C.B.

cresc.
mf
dim.
Velles et C.B.
Hb.
R
1o
pp
Cors en FA
arco
All° moderato 72=
poco marcato
pizz.
dim.

Maestoso 96 = ♩
1re Fl.
2e Fl.
Petite Fl.
Hb
1o
Cor Ang.
Cl.
Cl. B.
Bon
C. Bon
Changer en UT
Cors
Changer en UT
Tromp.
Tromb.
Timb.
Triangle
Cymb.
(Triangle Tacet)
Orgue
Maestoso 96 = ♩
à 2
ppp
pp
f
pizz.
arco
Col C.B.

Cors
Col C.B.

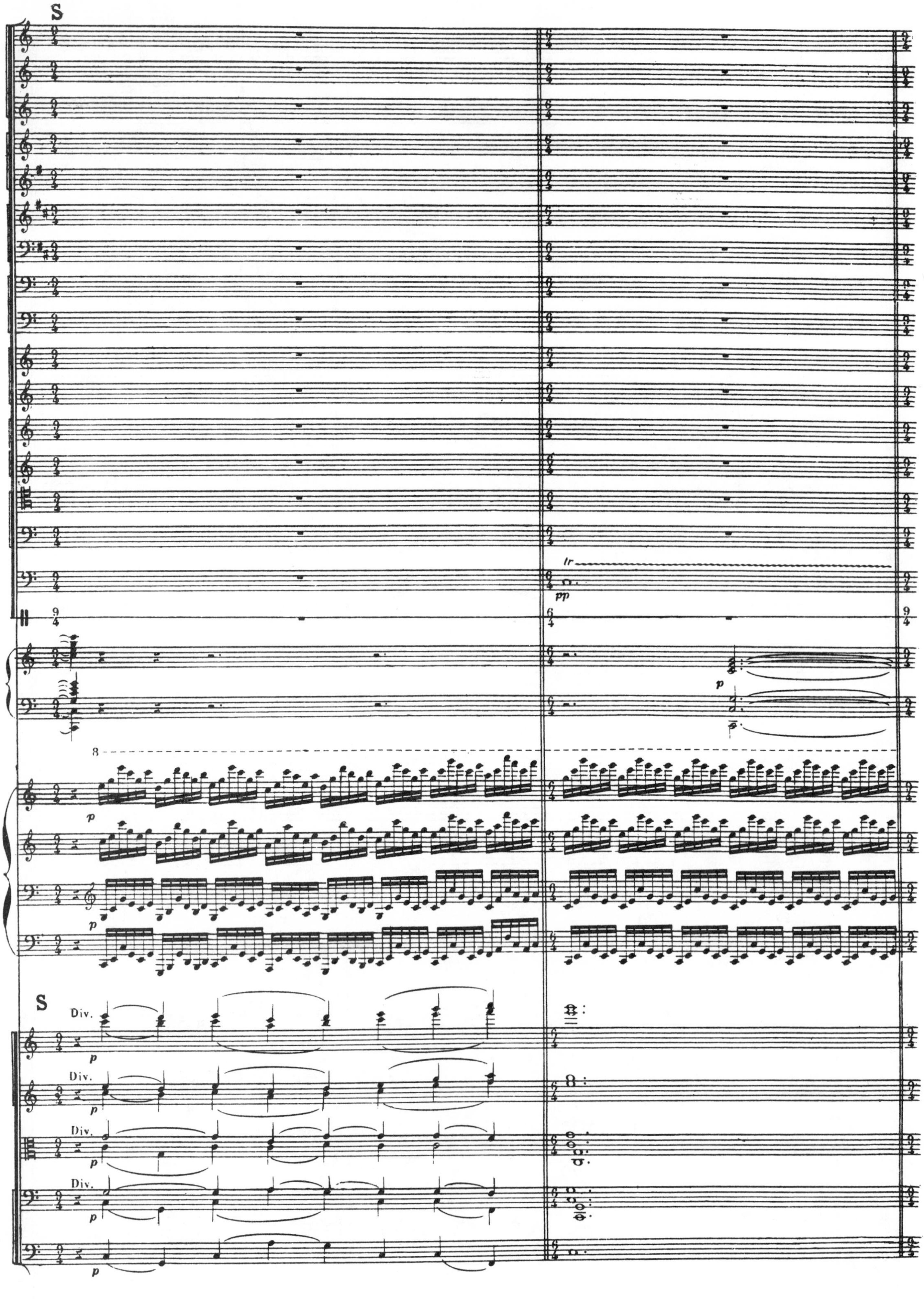
S
PIANO A 4 MAINS
S
Div.

tr
pp
p

tr
pp
p
8
Div.

tr
pp
p
8
Unis.

Cymb.
Unis
Unis
Unis
Unis

ff tr
ff tr

T Allegro 92 = 𝅗𝅥
Gsse Csse et Cymb.
ff
ff
tr
T Allegro 92 = 𝅗𝅥
f
f

à 2
à 2
à 2

U
à 2
1º
Div.
Unis.
Col C.B.

à 2
à 2
3e. Tromb.
Orgue
sempre f
sempre f
sempre f
pizz.
Col C.B.
sempre f
pizz.
sempre f

à 2
1º

V
mf espress.
1º
mf
mf
pp
V
pp
p
2ds Vons Div.
p
p
p

p
p
1º mf
mf
1º mf
p
cresc.
p cresc.
3º mf

f
1º f
2º
à 2
molto cresc.
cresc.

dim.
p
dim.
p
dim.
p
dim.
p
p
dim.
p
dim.
p
dim.
p
dim.
dim.
p

X
dim.
1º
p
3
2º
pp
3º
sons bouchés
ppp
Ped.
dim. Vlles Div.

pp
p
pp

Y
pp
p
Unis.
arco
pizz.

cresc.
à 2
mf
p
Col C.B.
arco

Z
1º
Col C.B.
Col C.B.
Z

à 2
Col C.B.

AA
f
à 2
Col C.B.

2º
2º
à 2
1º
à 2
f
ff

à 2
Orgue

à 2
Cymb.

à 2
ff
f
sempre f
senza Ped.
Div.
Unis.
Div.
Unis
Col C.B.

f
f
f
f
f
f
f
f
f
f

BB
1º
à 2
3º
f
BB

p
1º
pp Ped.
2ds Vons pp Div.
pp
Altos Div. pp
pp
pp
Div.
pizz. p

1º p
cresc.
p
cresc.
p
p
cresc.
pp
cresc.
cresc.
cresc.
cresc.

dim.
mf
dim.
4º
1º
tr
cresc.
Unis.
cresc
dim.

1º
2º
tr
pizz.

dim.
dim.
pp
dim.
p
ppp
pp

CC
p
3º
p
pp
CC
p arco

1º
p
1º
p
Unis.
Unis.
cresc.
cresc.
cresc.
p arco

cresc.
1º
cresc.
cresc.
cresc.
f
p
1er Tromb.
2e Tromb.
3e Tromb. et Tuba
cresc.

à 2
f
f
à 2
f
à 2
f
f

EE Sans presser
à 2
EE Sans presser

sf
sf

sf
sf

à 2
Unis.
Cymb.
Orgue
p
f
ff
sf

FF Stringendo
ff
cresc.
f
sf

Più All°. 138=𝅗𝅥
(une mesure comme trois du mouvt. précédent)
ff
à 2
tr
Cymb. et Gsse Csse
Ped.
Più All°. 138=𝅗𝅥
(une mesure comme trois du mouvt. précédent)

à 2
à 2
à 2
tr

stringendo
2°
2°
à 2
stringendo
8

à 2
1º
2º
3º Tromb.
Molto Allº 88=○
Div.
Unis
GG Pesante
Col C.B.
ff
sf

à 2
ff
tr
sf
100=𝅗𝅥 même valeur de mesure
Col C.B.

à 2
à 2
2º
ff
ff
3º Tromb.
ff
Col C.B.

100=𝅗𝅥 Sans presser
à 2
Cymb.
Orgue
ff
100=𝅗𝅥 Sans presser
sf
sf
Div.
Col C.B.

à 2
à 2
Unis
Col C.B.

Cymb et Gsse Csse
FIN

Dover Piano and Keyboard Editions

THE WELL-TEMPERED CLAVIER: Books I and II, Complete, Johann Sebastian Bach. All 48 preludes and fugues in all major and minor keys. Authoritative Bach-Gesellschaft edition. Explanation of ornaments in English, tempo indications, music corrections. 208pp. 9⅜ × 12¼. 24532-2 Pa. **$9.95**

KEYBOARD MUSIC, J. S. Bach. Bach-Gesellschaft edition. For harpsichord, piano, other keyboard instruments. English Suites, French Suites, Six Partitas, Goldberg Variations, Two-Part Inventions, Three-Part Sinfonias. 312pp. 8⅛ × 11. 22360-4 Pa. **$11.95**

ITALIAN CONCERTO, CHROMATIC FANTASIA AND FUGUE AND OTHER WORKS FOR KEYBOARD, Johann Sebastian Bach. Sixteen of Bach's best-known, most-performed and most-recorded works for the keyboard, reproduced from the authoritative Bach-Gesellschaft edition. 112pp. 9 × 12. 25387-2 Pa. **$8.95**

COMPLETE KEYBOARD TRANSCRIPTIONS OF CONCERTOS BY BAROQUE COMPOSERS, Johann Sebastian Bach. Sixteen concertos by Vivaldi, Telemann and others, transcribed for solo keyboard instruments. Bach-Gesellschaft edition. 128pp. 9⅜ × 12¼. 25529-8 Pa. **$8.95**

ORGAN MUSIC, J. S. Bach. Bach-Gesellschaft edition. 93 works. 6 Trio Sonatas, German Organ Mass, Orgelbüchlein, Six Schubler Chorales, 18 Choral Preludes. 357pp. 8⅛ × 11. 22359-0 Pa. **$12.95**

COMPLETE PRELUDES AND FUGUES FOR ORGAN, Johann Sebastian Bach. All 25 of Bach's complete sets of preludes and fugues (i.e. compositions written as pairs), from the authoritative Bach-Gesellschaft edition. 168pp. 8⅜ × 11. 24816-X Pa. **$9.95**

TOCCATAS, FANTASIAS, PASSACAGLIA AND OTHER WORKS FOR ORGAN, J. S. Bach. Over 20 best-loved works including Toccata and Fugue in D minor, BWV 565; Passacaglia and Fugue in C minor, BWV 582, many more. Bach-Gesellschaft edition. 176pp. 9 × 12. 25403-8 Pa. **$9.95**

TWO- AND THREE-PART INVENTIONS, J. S. Bach. Reproduction of original autograph ms. Edited by Eric Simon. 62pp. 8⅛ × 11. 21982-8 Pa. **$8.95**

THE 36 FANTASIAS FOR KEYBOARD, Georg Philipp Telemann. Graceful compositions by 18th-century master. 1923 Breslauer edition. 80pp. 8⅛ × 11. 25365-1 Pa. **$5.95**

GREAT KEYBOARD SONATAS, Carl Philipp Emanuel Bach. Comprehensive two-volume edition contains 51 sonatas by second, most important son of Johann Sebastian Bach. Originality, rich harmony, delicate workmanship. Authoritative French edition. Total of 384pp. 8⅜ × 11¼. Series I 24853-4 Pa. **$9.95**
Series II 24854-2 Pa. **$10.95**

KEYBOARD WORKS/Series One: Ordres I–XIII; Series Two: Ordres XIV–XXVII and Miscellaneous Pieces, François Couperin. Over 200 pieces. Reproduced directly from edition prepared by Johannes Brahms and Friedrich Chrysander. Total of 496pp. 8⅛ × 11.
Series I 25795-9 Pa. **$10.95**
Series II 25796-7 Pa. **$11.95**

KEYBOARD WORKS FOR SOLO INSTRUMENTS, G. F. Handel. 35 neglected works from Handel's vast oeuvre, originally jotted down as improvisations. Includes Eight Great Suites, others. New sequence. 174pp. 9⅜ × 12¼. 24338-9 Pa. **$9.95**

WORKS FOR ORGAN AND KEYBOARD, Jan Pieterszoon Sweelinck. Nearly all of early Dutch composer's difficult-to-find keyboard works. Chorale variations; toccatas, fantasias; variations on secular, dance tunes. Also, incomplete and/or modified works, plus fantasia by John Bull. 272pp. 9 × 12. 24935-2 Pa. **$12.95**

ORGAN WORKS, Dietrich Buxtehude. Complete organ works of extremely influential pre-Bach composer. Toccatas, preludes, chorales, more. Definitive Breitkopf & Härtel edition. 320pp. 8⅜ × 11¼. (Available in U.S. only) 25682-0 Pa. **$12.95**

THE FUGUES ON THE MAGNIFICAT FOR ORGAN OR KEYBOARD, Johann Pachelbel. 94 pieces representative of Pachelbel's magnificent contribution to keyboard composition; can be played on the organ, harpsichord or piano. 100pp. 9 × 12. (Available in U.S. only) 25037-7 Pa. **$7.95**

MY LADY NEVELLS BOOKE OF VIRGINAL MUSIC, William Byrd. 42 compositions in modern notation from 1591 ms. For any keyboard instrument. 245pp. 8⅛ × 11. 22246-2 Pa. **$13.95**

ELIZABETH ROGERS HIR VIRGINALL BOOKE, edited with calligraphy by Charles J. F. Cofone. All 112 pieces from noted 1656 manuscript, most never before published. Composers include Thomas Brewer, William Byrd, Orlando Gibbons, etc. 125pp. 9 × 12. 23138-0 Pa. **$10.95**

THE FITZWILLIAM VIRGINAL BOOK, edited by J. Fuller Maitland, W. B. Squire. Famous early 17th-century collection of keyboard music, 300 works by Morley, Byrd, Bull, Gibbons, etc. Modern notation. Total of 938pp. 8⅜ × 11. Two-vol. set. 21068-5, 21069-3 Pa. **$33.90**

GREAT KEYBOARD SONATAS, Series I and Series II, Domenico Scarlatti. 78 of the most popular sonatas reproduced from the G. Ricordi edition edited by Alessandro Longo. Total of 320pp. 8⅜ × 11¼.
Series I 24996-4 Pa. **$8.95**
Series II 25003-2 Pa. **$8.95**

SONATAS AND FANTASIES FOR THE PIANO, W. A. Mozart, edited by Nathan Broder. Finest, most accurate edition, based on autographs and earliest editions. 19 sonatas, plus Fantasy and Fugue in C, K.394, Fantasy in C Minor, K.396, Fantasy in D Minor, K.397. 352pp. 9 × 12. (Available in U.S. only) 25417-8 Pa. **$16.50**

COMPLETE PIANO SONATAS, Joseph Haydn. 52 sonatas reprinted from authoritative Breitkopf & Härtel edition. Extremely clear and readable; ample space for notes, analysis. 464pp. 9⅜ × 12¼.
24726-0 Pa. **$10.95**
24727-9 Pa. **$11.95**

BAGATELLES, RONDOS AND OTHER SHORTER WORKS FOR PIANO, Ludwig van Beethoven. Most popular and most performed shorter works, including Rondo a capriccio in G and Andante in F. Breitkopf & Härtel edition. 128pp. 9⅜ × 12¼. 25392-9 Pa. **$8.95**

COMPLETE VARIATIONS FOR SOLO PIANO, Ludwig van Beethoven. Contains all 21 sets of Beethoven's piano variations, including the extremely popular *Diabelli Variations, Op. 120.* 240pp. 9⅜ × 12¼. 25188-8 Pa. **$11.95**

COMPLETE PIANO SONATAS, Ludwig van Beethoven. All sonatas in fine Schenker edition, with fingering, analytical material. One of best modern editions. 615pp. 9 × 12. Two-vol. set. 23134-8, 23135-6 Pa. **$25.90**

COMPLETE SONATAS FOR PIANOFORTE SOLO, Franz Schubert. All 15 sonatas. Breitkopf and Härtel edition. 293pp. 9⅜ × 12¼. 22647-6 Pa. **$13.95**

DANCES FOR SOLO PIANO, Franz Schubert. Over 350 waltzes, minuets, landler, ecossaises, other charming, melodic dance compositions reprinted from the authoritative Breitkopf & Härtel edition. 192pp. 9⅜ × 12¼. 26107-7 Pa. **$10.95**

*Available from your music dealer or write for **free** Music Catalog to Dover Publications, Inc., Dept. MUBI, 31 East 2nd Street, Mineola, N.Y. 11501.*